Living
with an ...

EMO
KID

Charlie Mills

with Paul Tunis

Living

with an ...

EMO
KID

Charlie Mills

with Paul Tunis

RED ROCK PRESS   NEW YORK

To my eternally patient parents—Charlie Mills

Red Rock Press   New York, New York
www.RedRockPress.com

ISBN 9781933176-25-3

Copyright © 2009 in text: Charlie Mills
Copyright © 2009 in photographs: as listed below
Copyright © 2008: New Holland Publishers (UK) Ltd
This book first published in 2008 by New Holland Publishers
London • Cape Town • Sydney • Auckland

Library of Congress Cataloging-in-Publication Data

Mills, Charlie.
   Living with— an emo kid / by Charlie Mills.
      p. cm.
   ISBN 978-1-933176-25-3
   1. Parenting—Humor. 2. Music and teenagers. 3. Emo (Music)—Humor.
I. Title.
   PN6231.P2M555 2008
   818'.602--dc22

                          2008043440

American Editor: Paul Tunis
Senior Editor: Kate Parker
Editorial Direction: Rosemary Wilkinson
Production: Melanie Dowland

Cover design: Zoe Mellors and
Tom Hughes
Illustrations: Tom Hughes
Design: Zoe Mellors

Photographs (t=top, c=center, b=bottom): p30 © FoxSearch/Everett/Rex
Features; p32 © New Line/Everett/Rex Features; pp34 © ITV/Rex Features;
p35 © NBCUPHOTOBANK/Rex Features; p52 (b) © Rex Features; p53(c) Courtesy
of McCain-Palin 08; p53(t) Courtesy of Barack for America; p79(t) © iStock/Gary
Martin; p79(b) © iStock/Korshan Hasim Isik; p80(t) © iStock/Warwick Lister-Kaye;
p80(b) © iStock/Milos Luzanin; p81(t) © iStock/Michael Chen

Printed in Malaysia

CONTENTS

WHAT IS EMO?

And what has
it done to
this teenager?

"Emo" is short for **"emotional hardcore."**
Of course, it is. But what's that got to do with you?
Well, first you need to know that Emo is a music
genre specializing in aggressively loud rock with
amped-up angsty lyrics. "Emotionally-charged,"
if you will. Now, imagine you are a sunbeam
of a teenager, pootling through life and skipping
through piles of autumn leaves, then – SHABOOM
– you hear this music.

Something twists deep in your soul.
It is a clarion call, demanding you become …

Emo Kid.

If you are living with an Emo Kid, the most important thing you need to know is that Emo Kids are a social tribe whose members are finely in tune with their feelings. Trouble is, many of these emotions are different shades of the "living hell" variety, which means Emo Kids tend to smile even less than Henry Kissinger in a morgue. Sure, there are good times too, but the true Emo Kid prefers to slouch about under a near-permanent cloud of woe-is-me.

Obviously, gloom is a pretty stylish business. All that black, scowling and pouting is straight from the pages of *Vogue*. Also, Emo Kids are attuned to depths of misery, which ordinary mortals cannot begin to fathom. Yes, everyone has good cause to moan sometimes, but truly, life is tougher for floppy-haired teenagers. Without adult concerns like paying the mortgage and wondering if your nagging spouse is desperately itching to divorce you, there's nothing to focus on but your own personal misadventures. For Emo Kid, there is beauty in these dark emotions. Is hate not just baby-steps from love? Don't you get some of your most creative, bizarre and wonderfully crazed ideas when on the precipice of a doomed love affair? Isn't self-loathing a wonderful motivator? Don't you wish you could quit making "to do" lists and abandon yourself to thinking about memememememeee?

Each Emo Kid is a veritable vortex of feelings, which can prove a challenge for the most functional of house mates – even The Waltons would struggle to cope with an Emo Kid in their midst. Living with Emo Kid can prove the emotional equivalent of living with a black hole: froth and frivolity get sucked in and spat out quicker than you can say, "Cheer up, it might never happen," because it is happening. Right this minute.

Fortunately, this book is here to help. Learning the deeper meaning of Emo Kid's moany lyrics, circulation-constricting jeans and curious moods will score you brownie points beyond your wildest dreams. Emo Kid is a lot of fun when you know exactly what you're dealing with.

So start cherishing those anguished, "Nobody understands me!" wails you hear from behind Emo Kid's slammed-shut door, because by the time you reach the end of this book, you're going to be completely emotionally in tune with Emo Kid.

You might even turn a little bit emo yourself.

HOW TO SPOT AN
Emo Kid

The number one rule of being emo is not talking about emo. But if Emo Kid won't tell you that's what he or she is, how are you supposed to know if you're living with one?

		YES	NO
1	Does subject respond badly to helpful suggestions, like running a comb through the hair?	☐	☐
2	On any given day, is subject wearing more than five items of black clothing?	☐	☐
3	If you downloaded a Celine Dion album, thinking "You'll like this 'emotional' music: it's all about broken hearts," would you be risking violence?	☐	☐
4	Do you suspect subject enjoys looking so palpably downtrodden? Even a little bit?	☐	☐
5	Does hair in question get larger, in inverse proportion to the smallness of subject's spray-on jeans?	☐	☐

		YES	**NO**
6	Is it quite rare that subject looks at you, with both eyes, at one time? And without all that hair eclipsing the look?	❏	❏
7	If you walked into a room where subject was doing a celebratory jig, for reasons unbeknownst to you, would he or she stop as soon as you started clapping?	❏	❏
8	Does subject save the harshest judgment for Paris Hilton?	❏	❏
9	When listening to favorite music, does subject look saddened, bound up in own angst, irretrievably lost, or all three at once?	❏	❏
10	Do you feel tempted to book an osteopath appointment so a trained professional can drill subject in the importance of standing up straight?	❏	❏

If you answered YES to five or more of these, you are living with an Emo Kid.

BEING EMO:
The Rules

RULE 1

Don't call yourself Emo Kid. Leave that to everyone else.

RULE 2

Dress the part. Looking like an extra from *High School Musical* just isn't you.

RULE 3

Fall in love with someone inappropriate. It's hardly a story if you just get together, like each other, get married and live happily ever after, is it?

RULE 4

Keep a diary (you've got a high chance of turning it into a best-selling book. Misery memoirs really sell. You could call it *No One Understands Me and I Want to Die*).

RULE 5

If your doctor suggests that you wear looser fitting jeans, ignore this dubious advice. The jeans might be to blame for your unpleasant itch, but isn't suffering for love what it's all about?

RULE 6

Turn the volume up a notch higher. If more people listened to music as good as yours, the world might be a better place. They just need to get past the headache stage first.

RULE 7

Take time every day to prepare your most unamused face in anticipation for the day you might be trapped in an elevator with Will Ferrell, Jon Stewart and Jack Black.
Laughing is NOT emo.

RULE 8

You have a reputation for being sensitive so use it to your advantage … bursting into tears on a packed city bus will probably score you a seat.

RULE 9

If no one understands your poetry, take it as evidence you are a very special human being.

RULE 10

Start using a follicle-stimulating shampoo now. When hair is such a significant factor in your lifestyle, you can't afford to risk thinning in later life.

EMO EVOLUTION

How did that teenage
sunbeam become the
Emo Kid you live
with now?

STAGE 1

Smiley, happy, skippy
teenager. He walks with
a bounce and laughs himself
silly watching "The Simpsons."
He, at least, pretends to listen
to what you have to say, eats
dinner and sometimes even
says, "thank you." School is
OK, if only because it involves
a lot of larking around and
teachers accept it when he
occasionally "forgets" his
homework. He can be relied
upon to entertain the troops
at a gathering and is joyfully
unaware of the potential for
fun with the opposite sex.

STAGE 2

He attends a gig with some new friends from school and though he seems to have enjoyed himself, he walks differently afterwards. Slower. Droopier, perhaps—as if he's weighed down with thoughts and his mind is strolling along a street in a completely different world. He's not interested in introducing you to his new friends, regardless of how many heavy hints you drop. When he's not out with them, he increasingly spends his time shut alone in his bedroom and doesn't welcome you with open arms when you cheerily burst in. His hair has grown very long.

STAGE 3

His walk becomes a kind of lazy drag-and-stomp routine, which won't impress the judges on "Dancing with the Stars." Not that he is interested in watching that sparkle-fest any more. He switches the bass setting on his stereo from "clean" to "dirty," and the local drugstore cannot keep up with your demands for aspirin. His bangs are so long, you cannot look into his eyes. His skin looks paler, possibly because he hasn't been out in daylight for a long time. You suspect a romantic attachment but you have to contain your nosiness and not appear to pry, or you'll never extract any information on the topic whatsoever.

STAGE 4

When he finally gets tired of the bad jokes about his long shag, he hacks up his hair a bit with a rusty pair of garden shears, then irons the remnants straight. It doesn't improve matters much. But, hold on! His eyes look different. Is that eyeliner you see there? Hmmm. Whatever was going on in his love life, it's over now. But, weirdly, mourning over the lost love seems to take up more of his time than the relationship ever did. Instead of half-smiling pleasantly over the dinner table, he reads a slim volume of what looks like poetry as the rest of you eat.

STAGE 5

For a brief moment, the grand love affair is back on. He dyes a strand of his black hair electric pink. But then the soulmate rips out his heart and feeds it to a passing murder of crows. The ensuing plummet into hardcore emotion is dark and tortuous, but also peculiarly exhilarating. Emo Kid sets his self-penned poetry to music and uploads a blog to myspace. Then, just as you are preparing a speech urging him to get some fresh air and do something with his life, he is scouted on myspace and offered a multi-million dollar record deal.

LIVING WITH EMO KID:
DOs and DON'Ts

DOs

1   DO make sure there is at least one good mirror outside the bathroom, otherwise you are going to become uncontrollably enraged—and physically very uncomfortable—by the length of time Emo Kids take to style their hair in the morning.

2   DO be careful what you wish for. Begging Emo Kids to listen to that special music on their iPods instead of the stereo may mean you are spared the thrashy guitars, but any Emo Kid is still going to wail along out loud, which is somehow worse.

3   DO bake cupcakes. They are famous for giving even the sulkiest teenager a bit of child-like bounce. Particularly when covered with sugared up, synthetic icing and a crust of hundreds and thousands of sprinkles. We won't tell Jenny Craig if you don't.

4   DO play your own music as loud as your eardrums can take it, just for the satisfaction of having Emo Kid burst in and shout, "For the love of God, turn that racket down."

5   DO throw in your own, "You just don't understand me!" during a heated discussion with Emo Kid, because it totally wrongfoots them. Ditto, "It's so unfair!"

6   DO put a security code on your iTunes account, otherwise your credit card is going to melt with orders for new emo music.

7   DO invite well-meaning relatives over, as long as they promise to pinch Emo Kid's reluctant cheeks and say "Oooh, look how you've grown!" in a demeaning manner.

8   DO take advantage of Emo Kid's interest in death by getting him to bury your hamster when it dies. It is a horrible job, after all.

9   DO download REM's "Shiny Happy People" for your mobile ringtone and call yourself from the landline over and over again, to keep a buoyant mood in the house.

10 DO get a bouncing golden Labrador, so at least someone is pleased to see you when you come through the front door after a hard day.

DON'Ts

1   DON'T suggest Emo Kid dye a pink streak in hair to go
    better with the floral color scheme of the porch. Being emo
    is all about being nonconformist, silly.

2   DON'T bother making wisecracks like, "Where did you
    get that shirt, a garage sale?" because Emo Kid probably
    found it in that suitcase of your old clothes, and is wearing
    it with a healthy helping of irony. And a smirk, now.

3   DON'T be afraid to sneakily turn the electricity off at
    the circuit breaker and yell, "Oh no, a black out!" when you
    want Emo Kid to quit chatting to those mysterious online
    friends and help you rake leaves, or other chores.

4   DON'T offer to revive or start a tradition of reading
    aloud a bedtime story, just because Emo Kid has taken up
    an interest in literature. You are liable to get a slap.

5   DON'T steal Emo Kid's clothes for a Halloween party.
    It's not very supportive, is it?

6   DON'T think, even for a second, it's safe to leave Emo Kid
    alone for the weekend. He will miss you too much. Or, more
    likely, post an invite to a no-holds-barred party on myspace.

7   **DON'T** get a parrot for a pet, no matter how quiet
the house feels since Emo Kid took a vow of silence.
You will regret it when the parrot starts quoting Panic
At The Disco lyrics, throws itself off its perch and lies
on the floor, silently sobbing.

8   **DON'T** expect Emo Kid to take an interest in soft
furnishings, washing-up or bleaching the mold growing
in a damp corner of the bathroom. Emo Kids do not care
to sully themselves with such domestic drudgery. Unless,
of course, there are threats and / or money involved.

9   **DON'T** enter Emo Kid's lair without permission.
It's for your own safety.

10 **DON'T** feed Emo Kids alphabetti spaghetti then
expect them to eat the mournful poems just created
on the bowl's edge.

INSIDE EMO KID'S BEDROOM:
A Spotter's Guide

Unless you are the hapless roommate you don't often get the opportunity to get a good look at Emo Kid's bedroom, because privacy is so closely guarded. For the rare moments you are welcomed in (or sneak a peak while Emo Kid is out) here is what you can expect to find:

25

1   Stereo **The emo hub: the music is where emo all happens. If you have any electrical engineering know-how, see if you can adjust the speakers so they do not play quite so loud.**

2   Guitar **Was it not just yesterday that Emo Kid was having recorder lessons? At least the guitar has a lower shriek-factor.**

3   Furnishings **Notice anything, um, different here? Yes, the rug, curtains and walls are all as black and red as raven roadkill. You are cocooned in emo-ness. The effect is a bit spooky, but also very good for getting a nice peaceful snooze. It is comforting to know Emo Kid is well-rested. Only thoughts of white, hair-shedding cats and dogs keep Emo Kid awake at night.**

4   Wardrobe **More black, mixed with shades of onyx, charcoal and tar. A pair of pink and black striped tights dangling over the ceiling light like a nuclear reactor at night.**

5   Poetry **Inspiring verses might be written on the wall in—surely not!—blood, while other books sit stacked up all around the room. This is evidence of great intellect. Maybe.**

6   Hair dye **It is worth stocking up on 3-for-2 deals whenever you see them as a gift for Emo Kid. As long as the dye is black. There's nothing worse than having mousey roots growing into jet-black locks. "Mouse" is not a color of strong emotions, thus it is not emo. Black gets straight to the point.**

7 Eyeliner and nail polish **Despite knowing the shelf life of nail polish is improved when stored in the fridge, do not transfer it without Emo Kid's permission. However, if you recognize the eyeliner as one you purchased that mysteriously went missing, feel free to steal it back.**

8 Box of tissues **Emo Kids have a reputation for constant weeping. Though tears may be common currency in Emo Kid's world, it is more likely these are kept for a harmless morning nose-blow. Don't let the Kleenix alone convince you that Emo's suicidal.**

9 Posters **Emo bands, moody-looking landscapes, perhaps the odd picture of friends. What, no photographs of you? No problem: just give Emo Kid a portrait of yourself for Christmas. Who wouldn't want one!**

10 Computer **Technically, it's for school work. Research for papers and stuff like that. No one will ever know how much time Emo—or you, for that matter, spends working vs. chatting to friends online, downloading music and surfing peculiar websites.**

11 Unidentified Motionless Objects **Be careful of UMOs. Rubber gloves may not protect you. Heaven (or Hell, more likely) only knows what is in that pile or what planet it came from. Edge away very carefully.**

12 Notebooks **Or, more, interestingly, a top-secret diary. You cannot trust yourself to look inside. No, not even to touch it. Get out, get out!**

EMO POEMS:
Putting the "Poe" in Poetry

Music tames the savage beast, but not when the music is louder than a chainsaw.

How then can you ease Emo from a cranky fit? Get him to relax and stop wailing about how the world doesn't understand him. The secret weapon is ... poetry.

In case you haven't yet received your doctorate in romantic lit, here are some starter poems to quote in specific situations. But, if you cannot find the right emo verse to suit the occasion, just say what needs saying, mutter the name of a made-up poet and use Emo Kid's favorite put-down:

"You've probably never read that."

When Emo is a shattered, sobbing mess because his true love once again has run over his heart with a lawnmower, try this little number:

"If I can stop one heart from breaking,
I shall not live in vain:
If I can ease one life the aching,
Or cool one pain,
Or help one fainting robin
Unto his nest again,
I shall not live in vain."

—Emily Dickinson

"If I Can Stop One Heart From Breaking"

Usually Emo Kid is not feeling full of sunshine and buttercups when he arrives home after a long day at school. Serenade him with these poetic lyrics:

"A dark unfathom'd tide
Of interminable pride –
A mystery, and a dream,
Should my early life seem."

–Edgar Allan Poe
"Imitation"

Had enough of living with Emo Kid's gloom and doom?
Try out this:

"Bright star! would I were stedfast as thou art –
Not in lone splendour hung aloft the night
And watching with eternal lids apart,
Like nature's patient, sleepless Eremite,
The moving waters at their priestlike task
Of pure ablution round earth's human shores."

–John Keats
"Bright Star"

After Emo Kid emerges with a green tan from being holed in the dark for a week with only his computer monitor for company, he'll need quick emergency First Aid:

"Dar'st thou amid the varied
To live alone, an isolated thing?"

– Percy Bysshe Shelley
"The Solitary"

SEVEN SHADES OF EMO

Mirror, mirror, on the wall, who is the most emo of them all?

You might have noticed that Emo Kid will do anything to avoid the poisonous words, "You're just like me when I was your age." To that end, Emo Kid does his best to emulate these guys, whose emo-ness is scored in emo fringes.

DWAYNE HOOVER
from "Little Miss Sunshine"

7

Trapped in a dysfunctional suburban family, Dwayne escapes by taking a vow of silence for nine months in honor of his hero, Nietzsche. Dressed in a pair of black skinny jeans and a vintage band t-shirt, he communicates only by scrawling on a notepad and chalks off days on the wall like a prisoner counting time

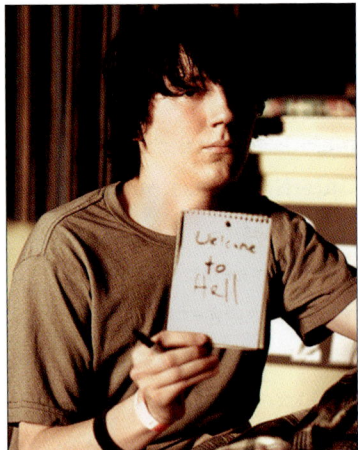

until the end of his sentence. He seems a bit sinister at first, but be patient and you will laugh yourself senile. It goes without saying Dwayne has big black floppy emo hair, a gorgeously lopey stride, and zero interest in winning any popularity contests at school. And his family? "No, you're not my family!" he screams at his mother, when he finally opens his mouth. "I don't wanna be your family! I hate you fucking people! Divorce? Bankrupt? Suicide? You're fucking losers, you're losers! No please just leave me here, Mom. Please, please, please. Please… just leave me here." Bless.

Emo rating: 7/7

MY CHEMICAL ROMANCE

Tricky: there are a lot of arguments about whether MCR are emo or not. Musically, My Chemical Romance has the heart, melody and the dark chaos. Furthermore, the lead singer, Gerard Way, has outstanding emo hair. It's either black (so classic) or dyed so platinum it's practically purple. Incredible. When he performs, Gerard gurns in the extreme, proving he runs the whole gamut of emo-tions. If that was not enough, Gerard has also publicly denied he and his band are emo. Not in the slightest. Everyone knows no true Emo Kid hires a plane to skywrite I AM EMO—true Emos just leave it to everyone else to

label them. Thus, My Chemical Romance is an emo group. Final. Damn them for going mainstream. Turning all stadium-emo dents their angsty credibility a little.

Emo rating: 6/7

TODD CLEARY
from "Wedding Crashers"

He could not fit in less with his family—a strict, upper-middle-class set who prize football-playing abilities, politics and girls in dresses. Todd's emo status is born as he sits painting at an easel while his relatives throw a ball around on the lawn of their great estate. His father urges him to join in ("It wouldn't kill you to play some competitive sports once in a while") and Todd, hair all over his face, stripey scarf flung around his neck screams, "Would that make you love me?" Perfect angst.

Emo rating: 5/7

JARED LETO,
actor/musician

Leto's emo status has always been in review. Starting off as a pop teen idol is usually the opposite of emo, but he was in "My So Called Life," a show that is a bible to Emo Kids everywhere. Later, Leto distanced himself from his emo roots with several gritty and tough roles in a number of indie films. But Leto returned to the fold in a big way with his band 30 Seconds to Mars. Shaggy black hair, loud / angsty lyrics, and make up? Check, check and check. But it's still hard to call Angelface from "Fight Club" full-emo.

Emo rating: 4/7

EMO PHILLIPS,
comedian

Well, he's called Emo, for a start. His hair looks pretty emo if you hold your head to one side and squint a bit. His humor is totally offbeat, which is good, but true Emo Kids are not in the business of making relentless wisecracks when they could be exploring and understanding their emotions instead of laughing at them. Plus, anyone who was born in the '50s can no longer be rightfully referred to as a "Kid."

Emo rating: 3/7

PETE WENTZ,
bassist, Fall Out Boy

Pete has the black floppy hair, the angsty sound and the right heartfelt / hardcore attitude. He even opened an emo-punk-themed beauty parlor—that's dedication to hairstyling. He is also a bit of a cutey, if that is your sort of thing. So far, so emo.

But marrying Ashlee Simpson dents his credibility more than confessing a clandestine Abercrombie & Fitch habit. Ashlee carries "It Bags." If that wasn't enough, her sister is Jessica Simpson, aka Breathing Barbie. That's a million miles from the spirit of emo, and then some. Minus points.

Emo rating: 2/7

CHARLES INGALLS
from "Little House on the Prairie"

Michael Landon, who played Charles, was known as Emo. Why? His real name was Eugene Maurice Orowitz. Rock and roll. He wasn't known for wearing punishingly tight jeans or listening to angst-tastic, heavy-hearted rock music—in his role as Pa Ingalls, he dressed in 19th-century farmer's gear and played the violin and mouth organ. At least he's a pioneer.

Emo rating: 1/7

WHAT NOT TO SAY
to Emo Kid

Everything you know about relating to fellow human beings is wrong.

Saying "You look nice," to Emo Kid is tantamount to a kick in the teeth because, however contrived the look is, however many hours it takes to throw that doomed effect together, it is not meant to look "nice." Nice is for preschool teachers and Meredith Viera. Nice is bland, boring, relentlessly mediocre. Nice is an insult.

"You'll always be Mommy's Little Angel to me."

"How is the sunshine of my life?"

"Whaddya say we all cozy up on the sofa and watch *Hairspray* tonight?"

The trouble is, social etiquette is so skewed in favor of niceness, it actually takes effort not to be nice. It's dangerously easy to trip up and send Emo Kid into a whirling dervish of despair. Watch out for these humdinging wrong 'uns:

"Do you want to talk about it?"

"I DO LIKE YOUR SWEATER. WHERE CAN I GET ONE LIKE THAT?"

"Wow, nice hair. Does it take a lot of product to make it look like that?"

"HOW WAS SCHOOL TODAY?"

"You said you wanted to go to Warped Tour, so I've bought a family ticket for all of us!"

"I know you love 'CHALLENGING' music, so I've signed you up for accordion lessons. Cool, huh?"

"Group hug! Group hug!"

"You're so cute when you smile"

"When was the last time we did something as a group? I know, let's all go for a walk."

"DO YOU REMEMBER WHEN YOU WERE LITTLE AND LOVED TO TAP DANCE?"

"I was just like you when I was your age."

"Why don't you invite your friends over for dinner this weekend? It would be great to really get to know them."

EMO STYLE AND GROOMING

This isn't about fashion: it's about identity.

Emo Kid dresses this way to be individual. Just like every other Emo Kid.

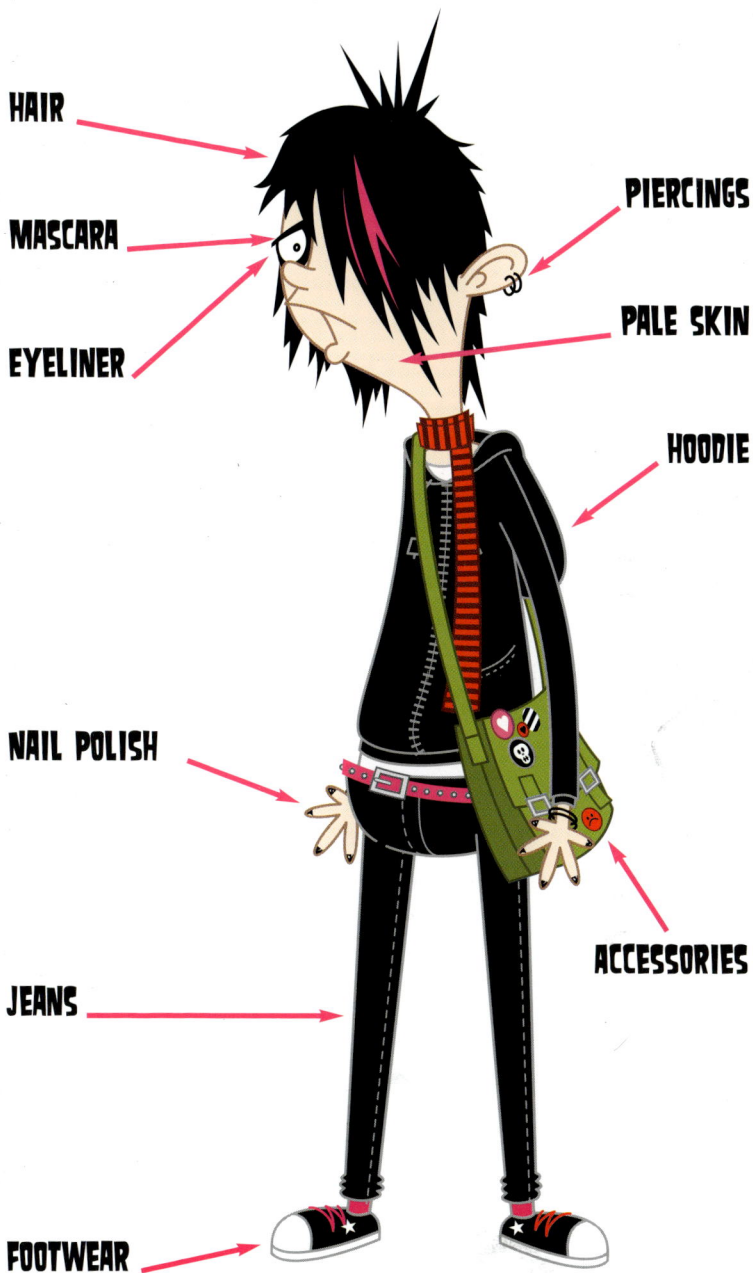

HAIR

MASCARA

EYELINER

PIERCINGS

PALE SKIN

HOODIE

NAIL POLISH

ACCESSORIES

JEANS

FOOTWEAR

Hair It's black, obviously. Ideally it would be naturally straight, perhaps even lanky enough to suggest a deficiency of fresh fruit and vegetables. However, some Emo Kids have been known to cheat and use straighteners to achieve the look. Such hair-styling tools are also used by the "Real Housewives of Orange County," so it is no surprise Emo Kid hides the straighteners. Pretend not to notice. In any case, Emo Kid will have a hard time registering the smirk on your face because it's so hard to see from behind those long, sweeping bangs. That hair hanging over the eyes is pretty much like a horse wearing blinders on a busy road, but Emo Kid would rather be 90 percent blind than deal with the world. If Emo Kids don't watch out for traffic and unexpected lampposts as they drag their heels down the street, a concussion or 100 percent blindness is in the cards.

Jeans Why so very, very tight? In years to come, historians will be more baffled by this than the mystery of how Stonehenge came to be. For now, all we know is that a pair of uncompromisingly skinny jeans makes "A Statement." In actual words, Emo Kids wear them because you do not. Pipecleaner-tight jeans have few redeeming qualities, being neither particularly flattering to the figure, comfortable or possessing pockets roomy enough to house spare change. Perhaps here we have the deepest reason for tight pants: being emo is about suffering, exposing your pain and being broke.

Hoodie **Tight, please, to emphasize the idea that Emo Kid is a grown person trapped in a child's body. The over-small hoodie will be worn all year round, regardless of the changing of the seasons. Ideally, this garment should remain unwashed during this time, thus generating Emo Kid's signature scent. C'mon, you can't expect to be deeply synched with your feelings with the dazzling smell of "spring glade" dryer sheets burning a path up your nostrils, can you? No. Impossible. The hoodie is the essence of emo.**

Accessories **Studded belts, leather cuffs, perhaps even a deep'n'meaningful *objet d'art* or inscribed pendant hanging from the neck by a frail leather strap—these are the essential grammar of emo style. If Emo Kid needs a bag, it's a messenger one, slung over the shoulder and across the body, and covered in patches and buttons. The rule of emo accessories is they require some reference to sensitivity (inscription: check) or suffering (studs: check). Anything else bestowed upon Emo Kid—diamond rings, Birkin bags—is liable to end up on eBay. Just so you know. However, a scarf is welcome because Emo Kid seems to live in a perpetual chill, and quilted vests tend to rob something from the Emo ensemble.**

Footwear **Close your eyes, and try to imagine your Emo Kid wearing tap dancing shoes or lime green Crocs. Doesn't work, does it? It completely ruins the mood. The fact is, Emo Kids spend a vast portion of the day looking down at their feet, so having a relentlessly jolly pair of shoes to gaze upon is plain distracting. That's why wearing a simple pair of Vans, black Converse, or a** stomping, chunky boot is so effective. However, anything you can buy in Nike Town is not welcome. One final note: flip-flops are not appropriate, not even black ones. The Emo walk involves copious scuffing of the toe, so the feet need protecting in order to avoid losing those precious digits. Without toes, there will be no more games of This Little Piggy Went to Market. Too cruel.

Pale skin The sun is Emo's enemy! Fake tan is Satan in bottled form! It helps if the skin isn't just a grayish pallor, but also has big dark circles under the eyes from all those late nights staying up reading tearjerking poetry or, er, headbanging. No bonus points for black eyes from said headbanging though: that's pushing the look too far.

Nail polish Smooth black varnish, as if the fingernails have been dipped in tar or the well of loneliness. Very dark red polish that gives the hands the appearance of an afternoon spent scrabbling around in dried blood is good, too. Chipped varnish and bitten nails work because they prove the wearer's sensitivity and suffering.

Eyeliner Pretty-pretty isn't the order of the day here. The black liner is not applied delicately, but as if the pencil was held in the fist of a particularly clumsy chimpanzee and then ringed around and around the eye in a deep, wild scrawl. It's a cry for help. An ancient proverb describes the eyes as "the window to the soul"—you have been warned.

Mascara **Oh, what dilemmas abound. Should Emo Kid wear waterproof mascara upon the lashes, because on any given day crying is very likely? Or non-waterproof so the face shows really dramatic evidence of weeping? Tricky decision. It's also worth knowing that waterproof mascara is very difficult to remove (bleach-based cleaning products are not recommended for the delicate eye area) so after several weeks of continuous wear, the lashes may actually get so weighed down they fuse the eye shut. Emo Kids get a kick out of being introverted.**

Piercings **Some Emo Kids look like a magnet loose in a paper clip factory. Ears, noses, eyebrows, lips, tongues, unmentionables— is nothing sacred? Such behavior cannot be encouraged, because otherwise airport scanners of the future will be on constant high alert. National security is at risk.**

8 REASONS TO RATE EMO GIRLS

Any fool knows
Emo Kids come in
both sexes.

We only say "he" in this book for the sake of
grammatical correctness and because "he or she"
takes too long to type. Androgyny may be the
order of the day, but some Emo Girls like to push
the envelope and should be applauded thus:

SHE MIXES MONROE WITH EMO

1

SHE EDUCATES ON GUYLINER MATTERS

2

SHE SETS THE BAR FOR MINIMAL EYE CONTACT

3

SHE HAS STEEL BELOW THE SURFACE AS WELL AS ON IT

4

SHE LIKES HER BOYS BEAUTIFUL

SHE RISES ABOVE THE DENIM WARS

6

SHE WILL NOT CATCH CHILL, DESPITE WEARING FEW CLOTHES

7

5

SHE MAKES ODD CLOTHES LOOK CHIC

8

1 **She mixes Monroe with Emo.** **Black hair is so ubiquitous in the emo world that if you want to stand out, you need a shot of Marilyn. Platinum blonde, please, not a pop princess shade of yellow, or you may as well cover yourself in fake tan and wear a Juicy velour tracksuit with "bad taste" embroidered across the bottom. So, yes, hair can be silvery, glow-in-the-dark blonde.**

2 **She educates on guyliner matters.** **Emo Girl has a key advantage over her male counterparts: better make-up. She would never make a rookie error like using a permanent marker pen to draw around her eyes, and she will advise her Emo Boy friends to procure themselves a nice, soft crayon-y kohl in order to stop looking like the Hamburgler.**

3 **She sets the bar for minimal eye contact.** **If Emo Guy requires 2/5 of the face to be covered by hair, Emo Girl goes for 3/5. A bigger hairdo to play with, you see. The less she makes eye contact, the easier it is for her to cultivate a bewitching air of mystery. Also, hiding behind that hair means she never gets inadvertently drawn into small talk about Britney Spears' early pop career and the like.**

4 **She has steel below the surface as well as on it.** **You might not immediately think Emo Girl is self-confident. Look again. She wears whatever she wants. If that's not proof she's got sass spilling from every pore, what is?**

She likes her boys beautiful. If Emo Girls liked their boys butch, you can bet Emo Boy would be out there building a neck so muscular it would resemble an elephant foot. We are all spared.

5

She rises above the Denim Wars. Seeing as Emo Boys work skinny jeans as well as, if not better than Heidi Klum. Emo Girls need a comeback. Tutus are the answer. Three good reasons: they're outrageous, girly, and outrageously girly.

6

She will not catch cold, despite wearing few clothes There is a rumor Emo Girls are trying to set a new world record for the amount of sweatbands, cuffs and brightly-colored bracelets worn between their wrists and elbows. Presently, this rumor is unverified. However, the good news for all those involved in this sport is that covering the wrists can keep the body about five per cent warmer, because the pulse point is protected from drafts.

7

She makes odd clothes look chic. Young ladies who are inclined to feel chilly may also be interested to know that fingerless gloves are bang on emo trend, particularly when worn indoors. Roomies who are looking for an excuse to turn down the thermostat, take note.

8

VICTORIA BECKHAM · EDWARD SCISSORHANDS

GLAMOROUS EMO GIRL

EMO VENN: GLAMOUROUS EMO GIRL

Emo Girl faces a nightmare situation. Basically, she wants a platinum blonde style, cut long and straight to frame the face, but cropped very short at the back. Any on-trend hairdresser knows this is a "Pob," the sharp blonde bob popularized by Posh Spice in autumn 2007. With such anti-emo spirits about, Emo Girl cannot risk a trip to the salon. Instead, she channels Edward Scissorhands and hacks up her hair in the privacy of her own home.

Or, your home. Whichever way you see it.

WARNING!

The Emo Cash Cow

A special note on band merchandise: underground music doesn't make very much money. There is nothing a crafty-minded band won't do to squeeze another buck out of the Emo Kid.

CAN ANYONE BE EMO?

Judge for yourself

The world would be a better place if everyone were in touch with their feelings. But can anyone carry off the look?
For example…

Emodonna

Bushmo

Emobama

Palinmo

Cagemo

EMO CINEMA
Morose movies

Emo Kid loves popcorn as much as everyone else, as long as it can be eaten in the dark of the movie theater, and he has time to retrieve the stray corns lost in his fringe.

Here are a few of Emo's favorite films.

Home Alone: Lost in New York	**Home Alone: Lost in Oneself**
The Devil Wears Prada	**The Devil Wears Black**
Highlander	**Highmaintenance**
Oceans 11	**Oceans of Tears**
Sweeney Todd	**Mopey Todd**
Brokeback Mountain	**Brokeback Moaning**
Shrek	**Shriek**
American Pie	**American Sigh**
PS I Love You	**PS I Hate You**
Tropic Thunder	**Tragic Whimper**

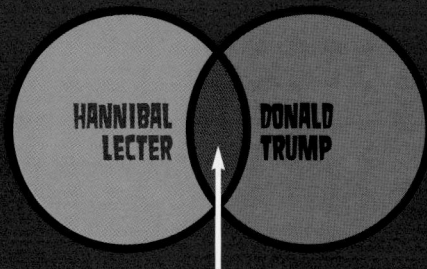

HANNIBAL LECTER

DONALD TRUMP

SCARY EMO KID

EMO VENN: SCARY EMO KID

With his best hair-growing years behind him,
Hannibal Lecter cannot hide his face behind a
mop of lank hair, so a hockey mask is brought in.
He is super-intelligent, alienated by society and
has a tenuous hold on sanity. Donald Trump
more than makes up for his fancy stiff hair with
some face-covering bangs and a hot temper to
boot. Plus he looks pretty respectable in a suit.
Scary Emo sits somewhere inbetween. Worrying.

EMO KID
In the Wild

Witnessing Emo Kid's behavior in your shared home can sometimes be disturbing. It makes you worry about what Emo Kid gets up to in the big wide world. No need to worry: spy away to your heart's delight right here...

In gig heaven. **Emo Kid probably has a guitar pick in his pocket, just in case the bassist is taken ill and a replacement is urgently needed. The dream may one day come true, but tonight Emo Kid is lost in the music. Or just plain lost. Emo Kid is not known for being the first one in the mosh pit—instead he watches in silent contemplation, feeling a shimmering shiver exude from the crowd as his heartstrings get plucked raw. If you are the designated driver who will take Emo Kid home, it is advised you sit outside in the car and wait politely instead of poking your head inside the venue and witnessing the screaming release of emotion in graphic technicolor.**

Soaking up coffee culture. **Funnily enough, Emo Kid's strict ethical code goes AWOL when in a hundred-yard radius of a Starbucks Frappucino. The only way Emo Kid can justify boosting the profits of a main-street homogenizing, corporate-cloning, soulless coffee shop is to sit there for hours with just a copy of *Descartes: Selected Philosophical Writings* for company.**

In that masterstroke, Emo Kid gets his depth back. And those frappucinos are mighty tasty.

Ripping open emotional veins. **Where better to pull open the wounds of unrequited love than at an underground poetry recital? Listening to fellow poets share their pain, ranting in angry seven-syllable verse and gently weeping through it all, pushes Emo Kid right to the verge of catharsis. But that is not wholly responsible for Emo Kid's new-found glow, no. That is down to the sweet, sweet knowledge that attending an underground poetry recital makes Emo Kid officially of a higher intellectual order.**

On the street. **OK, so Emo Kid is making a rare public appearance, but that does not mean he or she is anything but anti-social. What's an Emo Kid to do? The answer is obvious: shut out the world and tune into your feelings at the same time by listening to music. White iPod earplugs do the job, but wearing massive headphones scores big emo kudos, even if the pavement isn't wide enough to accommodate the armchair-sized speakers strapped to the side of Emo Kid's head. There is nothing about this look that encourages strangers or tedious neighbors to make conversation.**

Hanging out. **Deliberately vague, this. "Hanging out" could refer to sitting around chatting in a friend's room, scaring small children in parks or being eyed suspiciously by confused security guards in shopping centers. It is basically a description of doing Nothing Much Really, designed to worry oldsters.**

EMO:
Advice from verse

Have you ever thought, "That's it, I give in. Forget about me and my needs, just go out with your emo friends and have a great time (or a miserable one if you prefer)!" But of course, you do not lay your woes onto Emo Kid. If you care about them, set them free, hmm! This one is for you:

"While, like a ghastly rapid river,
Through the pale door
A hideous throng rush out forever
And laugh — but smile no more."

–Edgar Allan Poe
"The Haunted Palace"

For those quiet Sunday afternoons when you get sideswiped by a gory vision of the future, suddenly realizing Emo Kid could well be the person who chooses your nursing home:

*"Autumn wins you best by this its mute
Appeal to sympathy for its decay."*

–Robert Browning
"Paracelsus"

If you are hoping that Emo Kid is just going through a short-lived phase, quote this little nugget to reach out and bring him or her back from the dark side:

"My eyes are dim with childish tears,
My heart is idly stirred,
For the same sound is in my ears
Which in those days I heard.
Thus fares it still in our decay:
And yet the wiser mind
Mourns less for what age takes away
Than what it leaves behind."

—William Wordsworth
"The Fountain," *Lyrical Ballads*

Ideal for when all that loud music is playing late at night and you have to work in the morning:

"Sleep, sleep, beauty bright,
Dreaming o'er the joys of night.
Sleep, sleep: in thy sleep
Little sorrows sit and weep."

—William Blake
"A Cradle Song"

EMO KID

In Love

In a world populated by robots, Emo Kids are unashamedly romantic. An Emo Kid without an object of desire is like George Bush without something stupid to say: rudderless.

That's not to say every Emo Kid has a partner, no. In fact, emo relationships are best conducted at a distance. There is much more potential for miscommunication, misunderstanding and unfulfilled yearning—the very lifeblood of emo existence.

Emo Kids are so full of feeling they fall in love very easily. It is possible for Emo Kid to extract "A Moment" from an exchange with a cashier in Dress Barn. In Emo world, it does not take much to get a grand love affair going.

One sideways look, another carefully-timed blink, perhaps even a cold shoulder. This evidence points in one direction only: love. Strike up a classic emo tune into the background and Emo Kid's heart is signed, sealed and delivered.

Emo Kid is not afraid to say "I love you." and at any given moment can be found musing on a new poem for his or her loved one. Emo Kid would never use "I LUV U" text-speak when a 12-page handwritten love letter would do. An Emo is only a hop, skip and a jump away from leaping up and down on Oprah's sofa.

Given Emo Kid's sensitivity, you might be surprised to know emo music is more famous for angry tunes than soppy love songs, but really the two are one and the same. Take "I Don't Love You" by My Chemical Romance, for example. It tells the story of a girl breaking up with her boyfriend. He is destroyed and angry, which makes what he has to say profound and poetic. With rage, passion and dejection defining every syllable, he challenges the girl to say, "I don't love you / Like I did / Yesterday"—a line that does not so much tug at the heartstrings as rip them right out.

But, as the slogan on one special emo T-shirt says, "Prose before hos." The message being, it is better to have an eloquent grasp of the English language than to have your true love by your side. Otherwise, you and your loved one are headed for a life of domestic bliss in a cute little cottage with roses round the door, which is the least emo thing in the world.

THE EMO
Hate Parade

It might seem Emo Kid is just plain miserable all the time, but that's not the case.

True Emo Kids are those who experience deeper emotions than other people, and aren't afraid to show them. Isn't it better to deal with your darkest emotions rather than bottle them up until eventually they spew out of your rectum? You need to know the nuances and shades of every mood to really understand Emo Kid. Use this as your introduction.

Life is not all hugs and puppies, sadly. Normal, everyday things like catching sight of Simon Cowell on the TV can really get Emo Kid down. That man not only gives black t-shirts a bad name, but he is also responsible for force-feeding an audience seriously wretched music. His work on "American Idol" makes him the high priest of pop puppets and it is distressing to see so many people buying his records and—worse—making up to him. So arrogant! So smug! Such appalling trousers! Complete anti-emo.

Black Cloud rating: 3

While magazines are a great way for Emo Kid to keep up on music and fashion, or even plan their future full-body tattoos Teeny Bobber Magazines are dead to rites. The foldout posters of High School Musical stars are deeply offensive. Beware: these magazines are not to be brought within a five-foot proximity of Emo Kid, or the glossy pages of teen idol celebrity gossip will spontaneously combust in your hand.

Black Cloud rating: 5

School is some sort of sick popularity contest. Occasionally an English or Art class might capture Emo Kid's imagination, but that cannot compensate for the idiots who drag their knuckles around the halls. Sometimes it would actually be preferable to spend one's time trapped in a hot elevator full of people with unfortunate digestive problems than inside the school gates.

Black Cloud rating: 4

If school is unsafe, the outside world is not much better. First problem: rain. It is good the universe can show its emotions with a cathartic weeping session, but rain causes havoc with the hair. Even if Emo Kid whips up a hood in time, the moisture in the atmosphere can cause carefully-straightened hair to expand like a ragged sponge in a sink.

Black Cloud rating: 5

Other cosmetic worries, like running out of eyeliner and hair that falls out due to overuse of straighteners and abrasive dye, can cause sleepless nights that only contribute to the wretched state of affairs.

Black Cloud rating: 4

Thankfully Emo Kid goes through emotions with astonishing speed, so these storm clouds do not take long to blow over. Be warned though: any loved-one who crosses Emo Kid during one of these above-mentioned episodes can expect things to end badly. Sorry about that.

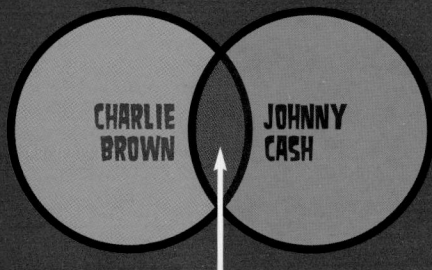

CHARLIE BROWN   JOHNNY CASH

"GOOD GRIEF" EMO KID

EMO VENN: "GOOD GRIEF" EMO KID

There is plenty for the Emo Kid to be down about. The world is a constantly bleak affair, not to mention that someone is always ready to pull that football away right before you kick it; worst of all that same person is your psychiatrist (I guess that's what you get for a nickel). The "Good Grief" Emo has the blues but he wouldn't be caught dead in a loose, traffic-yellow shirt, so he pulls a page from the "man in black."

HOW TO
Embarrass Emo Kid

It is hard to tell whether Emo Kids are antagonistic or self-effacing. Embarrass them and find out their true mettle. It's worth having a rapid exit strategy planned well in advance, but you will enjoy seeing how far you can push it.

STAGE 1:

Play "Take On Me" at top volume, and loudly ask Emo Kid to please turn the music down. How does that go down?

STAGE 2:

Turn up at school during Emo Kid's lunch break to deliver a hug. Don't let go. Nice?

STAGE 3:

In secret, buy tickets for the My Chemical Romance tour and turn up wearing your best beige slacks. When you see Emo Kid, say, "Hey dude, fancy seeing you here!" Success?

STAGE 4:

Sign Emo Kid up for a part in the community theater. Drama is a great way to express those emotions, after all. Is playing Cinderella the highlight of Emo Kid's life so far?

STAGE 5:

Pack Emo Kid off to polo lessons so you can loudly tell everyone that he is new-best-friends with the Hilton sisters. Fnar fnar. Is he proud?

STAGE 6:

Join Emo Kid's therapy group so you can really get to know each other in a right-on manner. Do you break through?

STAGE 7:

Call to arrange a surprise makeover for Emo Kid. On primetime TV. Does he or she call child protective services to complain?

STAGE 8:

Launch an Emo & Buddy beauty pageant to show your support for Emo Kid's style. Is this the beginning of something beautiful?

STAGE 9:

Organize a stripper for Emo Kid's 18th birthday party. Has he filed for divorce yet?

STAGE 10:

Wear your pants on your head. All teens love that. Don't they?

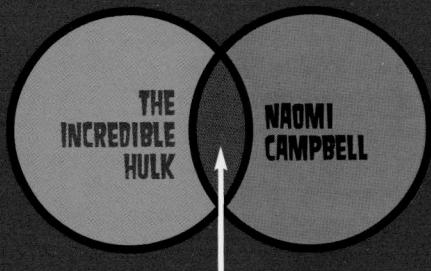

THE INCREDIBLE HULK — NAOMI CAMPBELL

TESTY EMO KID

EMO VENN: TESTY EMO KID

"You wouldn't like me when I get angry." The Testy Emo has the Hulk's capacity for angsty rage. Perfectly emo, if only his shaggy hair wasn't so green and his purple shorts so loose. Supermodel Naomi Campbell may have a temper you would not like to be shut in a soundproofed room with, but at least she dresses well, as shown when she turned up for community service wearing couture clothing. Testy Emo Kid sits bang between the two.

HAPPY BIRTHDAY,
Emo Kid!

While birthdays are traditionally a celebration of another year of life, Emo Kid has a grim spin: Every birthday brings you closer to death.

For those who love nothing better than planning a good ol' bash, you are advised not to stand outside the college gate with a bunch of balloons handing out invitations to Emo Kid's birthday. Not every classmate is a friend. Hijacking Emo Kid's myspace and inviting his 1,371 online "friends" to come out and play is not a good idea, either.

There is a chance Emo Kid may not want you involved at all
in birthday planning. Unless you would like to purchase a crate
of tooth-tingly sweet winecoolers, in which case you may be

permitted to deliver the goodies to the front door while Emo Kid's real friends—those he or she doesn't live with—do emo things in your house. The neighbors may wonder what is going on as you forlornly stand outside, looking through your own living room window, but c'est la vie.

However, being miserable is not your specialty—you are not the Emo Kid in this residence. So don't moon around, step right in to the more familiar role Miss or Mr. Congenialty. Get everyone together, even if you have never before sustained a conversation of more than five minutes with any of them.

You'll need to bake a cake for the occasion. Emo the offering up a bit by icing it black, and piping a few chilling lines of poetry on the top. Better still, make it a few months before the big day, so the gateau is as cobwebbed and moldy as Miss Haversham's wedding cake. She is the Emo Mother—you have to admire her decades-long commitment to doing nothing but sitting around and weeping through her heartbreak.

NOTE: PLEASE TAKE EXTRA CARE WITH BIRTHDAY CAKE CANDLES.

Emo bangs are notoriously long and there is nothing like the stench of burnt hair to sour the birthday celebrations, never mind the trauma of having short, patchy hair like a wigless Joan Collins. Poor Emo Kid.

PRESENT WISH-LIST *

- "Curious Hearts" —new fragrance from Britney, which presumably smells of stale champagne and fake tan

- A pair of tickets to see *Lord of the Dance*

- A large, bright sweatshirt with "Abercrombie & Fitch" emblazoned upon the chest in large, shouty letters

- A handbag-sized pooch in a Louis Vuitton carry-case. Maybe a diamond studded leash as well, for running the little ferrety fella around the park

- A lifetime subscription to *US Weekly!*

* THE AUTHOR CANNOT ACCEPT RESPONSIBILITY FOR EMO KID'S SATISFACTION WITH THESE GIFTS. YOU FOOL.

EMO KID

on Vacation

It is traditional for families to have a getaway together every year. These trips are so deeply embedded in our culture that many people view a week in the sun as a human right. Emo culture, however, sees things rather differently. A family vacation involves being separated from friends, having no privacy and being surrounded by the sort of people Emo Kid usually takes great pains to avoid.

BUT NO MATTER.
YOU ARE ALL GOING ON A TRIP AND THAT IS THAT.

Any trip that crosses more than a state or province line has special hurdles. The first is getting through customs. No, not because Emo Kid has made it onto INS's Most Wanted list, but simply because Emo no longer looks anything like his or her smiling passport photo. Customs officers tend to be suspicious of people who cover their whole face with hair. Suggest Emo Kid goes for a more pulled-back look, just until the border is behind you.

But should you really head south? The beach vacation may not be the exotic paradise for Emo Kid that it is for you. Admittedly, sweating so much your eyeliner runs is pretty undignified. And because Emo Kid is so unused to bright light, a single day of sunbathing will turn his skin into something resembling Russian borscht, that is, beet soup.

EMO PACKING ESSENTIALS:

- industrial-strength sunscreen

- swimming cap
  (frizzy hair must be avoided at
  all costs)

- Vaseline
  (in the heat, drainpipe jeans can
  actually become welded to the leg)

- iPod, plus the largest, most anti-
  social speakers the airline's baggage
  allowance will permit

- waterproof eyeliner

What about going away to sea? A cruise is one option: it certainly offers more breeze than the beach. Emo Kid might even make friends with the on-board entertainers—they are definitely unafraid to express themselves. Very Emo. If only cruise ship entertainers weren't so fond of using "jazz hands" to show their emotions.

Sailing is also a possibility, though it will be hard for Emo Kid to shout, "Leave me alone," with any authenticity when you are all trapped on a boat roughly the size of a Volvo.

If you are secretly hoping your Emo Kid will shed the high-maintenance beauty routine, take him or her camping. Once Emo Kids discover there is nowhere to plug in the straighteners, they might ease up a bit. Who knows? You might even bond over the last wet wipe. Maybe.

National Parks, often considered an easy option for families, offer something for everyone. While you tramp on the forest trails, splash around on the lake and get bathing suit burns on the splintery dock, Emo Kid will certainly enjoy pouring scorn on the whole thing, sure of getting emo points for being such a nonconformist among the fun-by-numbers drones. Like you.

Skiing is a potential activity in the winter. It scores for being cold and the fact black looks really good against the snow. Hurtling downhill into an ice-laden headwind isn't going to do Emo's hair any favors, but if you opt for the ski resort of Emo in Ontario, the kid might just forgive you for it.

ENCOURAGING
Positive Thinking

Sharing premises with Emo Kid can make you want to shout: "Enough of this, 'Nobody will ever love me,' malarkey." Worried, you realize it's time to harness the power of positive thinking and pump up Emo Kid's self-esteem. Success is all about attitude. Heck, if Dorthory only needed to wish herself home from Oz, who knows what positive thinking could do for the Emo Kid.

Unfortunately, an innate emo quality is the ability to believe the worst in everything. Challenge Emo Kid to face the happy truth with the following simple quiz—the more NOs he scores, the greater the proof that good things can happen.

		YES	**NO**

This is
your bicycle...

1 Does a dog lift his leg and pee on it? ❑ ❑

Does anyone steal your bicycle? ❑ ❑

Do you forget which railing you
chained your bicycle to and have
to walk home in the rain? ❑ ❑

You decide
to cut your
own hair...

2 Do you end up looking like your mother? ❑ ❑

Does your mother scold you as severely
as she did the last time you cut your
own hair, aged four? ❑ ❑

Do you now get mistaken for Rudy
Giuliani from behind? ❑ ❑

| | YES | NO |

It's time for a shower...

3 Do you get slashed to death by a crazy transvestite, like in *Psycho*?   ❏ ❏

Do frogs pour out of the shower head?   ❏ ❏

Do you slip over and paralyze yourself from the waist down, thus making it very difficult for you to shoehorn yourself into skinny jeans?   ❏ ❏

You get a new cell phone for your birthday...

4 Does your phone melt with the amount of emotion pouring through it?   ❏ ❏

Does your ringtone switch itself to something by James Blunt?   ❏ ❏

Does it throw itself out of the window?   ❏ ❏

	YES	NO

This kitten is yours...

5   Does it meow brightly and give you
    a sinister cat smile when you ask,
    "Why does everyone hate me?"   ❏   ❏

    Does it spill your boiling-hot cup of
    coffee over your face, causing a scar
    that looks like a purple moustache?   ❏   ❏

    Does it leap from your arms into the
    canal, making it look as if you were
    trying to drown it deliberately?   ❏   ❏

There we have it: proof the world is a
happy, smiling place. What's to be sad about?

EMO POEMS:

Advice from verse

Having trouble explaining to Emo Kid why he should get a job if he wants to buy those concert tickets instead of borrowing your credit card? Try this:

"The keenest pangs the wretched find
Are rapture to the dreary void,
The leafless desert of the mind,
The waste of feelings unemployed."

—Lord Byron
"The Giaour"

When Emo Kid has been taking the whole gloomy thing a bit too far:

"Better by far you should forget and smile
Than that you should remember and be sad."

—Christina Rosetti: "Remember"

Want to see your Emo crack a smile? Try this one:

"Razors pain you;
Rivers are damp;
Acids stain you;
And drugs cause cramp.
Guns aren't lawful;
Nooses give;
Gas smells awful;
You might as well live."

—Dorothy Parker
"Resume"

You didn't think Emo Kid would mind if you painted the walls of his room white to lighten him up. Use this line to coax him out of the linen closet:

"White shall not neutralize the black, nor good
Compensate bad in man, absolve him so:
Life's business being just the terrible choice."

—Robert Browning
"The Ring and the Book"

WHAT'S GOING ON...

... inside Emo Kid's Head?

Will my love ever recognize my existence?

How many piercings can I fit on my face?

Is that rain cloud following me?

Why are my parents so square?

Does my hair look ok?

How has that bully not been straight-jacketed and wheeled out of my life already?

Why is the pigeon looking at me like that?

Who buys Snoop Dogg records?

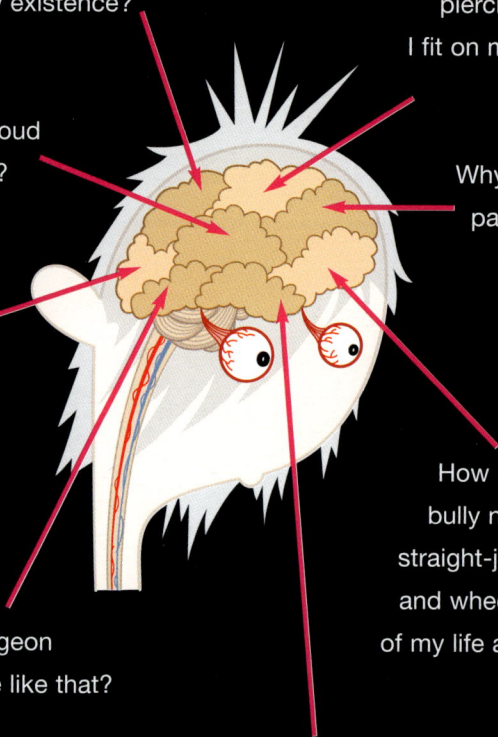

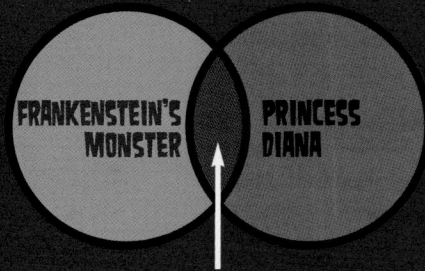

FRANKENSTEIN'S MONSTER — PRINCESS DIANA

MISUNDERSTOOD EMO KID

EMO VENN: MISUNDERSTOOD EMO KID

Frankenstein's Monster is created by a man with little idea of how to cherish his nearest and dearest. FM is abandoned and forced to spend his life on the run from the turnip-heads who persecute him. FM is desperate to find someone who will understand him and love him for who he is. Princess Diana had a similar story, but she had the advantages of good cheekbones and a strong fashion sense. Obvious emo middle-ground here.

COMMUNICATION

Tips

Sometimes Emo Kid can be hard to talk to. Shyness, thoughtfulness and introversion are key elements of emo.

Try this script to kick-start a conversation:

"All the better for talking to you"

Makes mournful growling sound, like a polar bear on the last remaining iceberg

"Wait a sec, I'll just grab my rain boots"

"You're so understanding. I love you so much I think I might burst"

Whips off emo wig and says, "I love you too!"

Emo Kid is possibly being sarcastic, but nevertheless this is the nicest conversation you've had with them in weeks. Quit while you're ahead.

"Hey, young scamp, how are you? Is this a good time to talk?"

Feigns deafness → return to beginning, repeat louder

Yes

No

"I am sorry to hear that. When is good for you?"

"I was just wondering how you were feeling today?"

"Terrible"

Hides behind hair

"When I'm dead"

"Please, tell me how I can help"

"Oh, come on, there's nothing some cookies and milk can't solve."

"Give me some money"

"Leave me alone"

"I believe it was The Beatles who sang 'Money Can't Buy You Love' and they were dead right. Maybe you and I could go for a nice walk, instead?"

"I hate you"

"You got any cyanide?"

"You're difficult. I love that about you. Grrr!"

Leaves room

Calls Childline, begging for help

Calls local psychiatric hospital and is heard saying, "I can hold this lunatic until you get here. Please hurry."

Please note: the author has made every effort to ensure that the information given in this book is safe and accurate, but cannot accept liability for any resulting law suit, filial divorce or injury caused by cranky Emo Kid. Quit now.

THERE — DOESN'T BONDING FEEL GREAT?

THE CIRCLE OF TRUST
Emo Kid's friends

Emo Kids might seem quiet or shy, but in the right company they are wild social animals and will openly divulge deeply personal secrets. If you want to really connect with Emo Kid then you must maneuver yourself into a position where you join the circle of trust.

Though the Emo Kid you live with may sometimes seem uncommunicative or hostile, he or she has another side. Typically, teenagers are rude and foul-mouthed at home yet oddly full of sweetness and light with outsiders, particularly with a friend's parents. Take advantage of this.

DO NOT BE AFRAID TO BUY FRIENDSHIP.

Welcome Emo's gang into your home with chocolate and free reign on the remote control.

Watch for the friend wearing pants that enable the blood in the legs to circulate freely. This person is clearly less committed to the emo cause. You want your Emo Kid to become closer to this friend. Inevitably there will be one or two friends in the crowd who arouse your suspicions—perhaps they are pierced in a few too many locales, look like thieves or appear stark, raving mad. However, warning your Emo Kid against these characters will only backfire.

Offering invaluable domestic services like drink-pouring and late-night chauffeuring will score you brownie points with the group. Soon enough, they will feel comfortable in your company. When you hear a little nugget like,

"So when are you having that party?"

or "How far have you got, *you know?*" do not flinch.

Extract more information by positioning yourself next to the front door, 24/7, so you are always there to answer the doorbell when a member of Emo Kid's gang comes by. Welcome friends in, insist they make themselves comfortable, offer nibbles, and do not, under any circumstance, call upstairs to Emo Kid until everyone is settled

in conversation with you. Emo Kid then has no choice but to join in. Feel free to ask questions like,

"So where did you get the money for those festival tickets?"

and actually get answers.

CONGRATULATIONS, SPECIAL AGENT EMO:

you have infiltrated the circle of trust.

EMO KID

In the Future

Unfortunately, Emo Kid's days are numbered. No, the Grim Reaper is not hovering above his head (though sometimes Emo Kid might wish it was).

At some point, Emo Kid is going to turn

30

and be forced to make some adult decisions, like getting a job.

Can you imagine Emo Kid slipping into a hot bubble bath to read the latest James Patterson after a busy day at work? It could happen. And Emo Kid may have spent all day doing something like this...

ACCOUNTANT

Expert at telling the IRS his clients are misunderstood. Frequently heard shouting, "Why are you being so unfair!" down the phone at the end of every financial year.

TRAFFIC COP

Often heard screaming, "Why do you hate me?" at people whom he has just ticketed, then is seen smiling as he zooms away.

TEACHER

Emo Teachers revisit the classroom nightmares that shaped them and are hellbent on sending the anti-emos into everlasting detention.

SURGEON

Behind that mask, who knows what Emo Surgeon is feeling? Patients who wake up mid-operation and see Emo hovering above with a scalpel in hand may suffer shock-induced heart attacks.

SOCIAL WORKER

Spending every day in the company of seriously dysfunctional families makes his or her own teenage years seem relatively normal. No, no, they were hell.

COSMETICIAN

All those years of practice with guyliner pay off at last. Tattoo territory beckons.

PSYCHIATRIST

Just for fun.

COULD I
Be Emo?

The whole emo thing isn't so scary now, is it! Feeling like all this research has changed something deep within you? Put you in touch with your emotional core?

Ultimately, it is all about being true to yourself. Stop pressuring yourself to be perfect—now it is time to focus on rebuilding your life from the ashes of your mistakes. Wear the clothes that really say something about who you are and what you are feeling at the moment.
Be true! Be emo!